INSIDE THE WORLD OF SPORTS

BASKETBALL

INSIDE THE WORLD OF SPORTS

AUTO RACING
BASEBALL
BASKETBALL
EXTREME SPORTS
FOOTBALL
GOLF
GYMNASTICS
ICE HOCKEY
LACROSSE
SOCCER
TENNIS
TRACK & FIELD
WRESTLING

INSIDE THE WORLD OF SPORTS

BASKETBALL

by Andrew Luke

MASON CREST

Mason Crest
450 Parkway Drive, Suite D
Broomall, Pennsylvania 19008
(866) MCP-BOOK (toll free)

First printing
9 8 7 6 5 4 3 2 1

Names: Luke, Andrew, author.
Title: Basketball / Andrew Luke.
Description: Broomall, Pennsylvania : Mason Crest, [2017] | Series: Inside
 the world of sports | Includes index.
Identifiers: LCCN 2015046235 (print) | LCCN 2016015607 (ebook) | ISBN
 9781422234587 (hardback) | ISBN 9781422234556 (series) | ISBN
 9781422284209 (ebook) | ISBN 9781422284209 (eBook)
Subjects: LCSH: Basketball--United States--History.
Classification: LCC GV883 .L85 2017 (print) | LCC GV883 (ebook) | DDC
 796.3230973--dc23
LC record available at https://lccn.loc.gov/2015046235

QR CODES AND LINKS TO THIRD-PARTY CONTENT

CONTENTS

KEY ICONS TO LOOK FOR:

Words to understand: These words with their easy-to-understand definitions will increase the reader's understanding of the text while building vocabulary skills.

Educational Videos: Readers can view videos by scanning our QR codes, providing them with additional educational content to supplement the text. Examples include news coverage, moments in history, speeches, iconic sports moments and much more!

Text-dependent questions: These questions send the reader back to the text for more careful attention to the evidence presented there.

Research projects: Readers are pointed toward areas of further inquiry connected to each chapter. Suggestions are provided for projects that encourage deeper research and analysis.

The Larry O'Brien NBA Championship Trophy, named for a past commissioner of the league, made its debut in 1977. Each year a new trophy is made at the cost of about $13,500.

CHAPTER 1

BASKETBALL'S GREATEST MOMENTS

Basketball is a purely American game. It has become popular in countries all over the world, but basketball was born and bred in the United States.

Before blossoming into the multibillion-dollar enterprise that is the National Basketball Association (NBA), basketball matured at the college level. This book focuses on the professional level, but in basketball, the sport was far more popular as a college game before pro basketball gained any traction with the sport's fans.

The first college basketball game was held in the 1890s, some 50 years before the NBA existed. By the 1920s, there were eight major conferences of basketball-playing schools. The first National Invitation Tournament was held in 1922 in Indianapolis, Indiana, and won by Wabash College. Now one of the most popular and lucrative sporting events in the country, the National Collegiate Athletic Association (NCAA) Men's Basketball Tournament was established in 1939.

Women have played basketball from its years of origin as well, also beginning at the collegiate level. The first intercollegiate women's game took place between Stanford and California in 1896. Women's basketball was added to the Olympic Games in 1924. The first intercollegiate women's national championship game was played in 1967, with the first NCAA Women's Basketball Tournament held in 1982.

The NCAA Men's Basketball Tournament has produced many memorable basketball moments over the decades, from North Carolina State's upset win over the University of Houston in 1983 to Christian Laettner breaking Kentucky's heart at the buzzer in 1992. There was the historic 1966 victory by Texas Western over a Kentucky team that was its opposite in every way. And before Michael Jordan became the best player on the planet, he foreshadowed his clutch shot-making ability to win North Carolina a championship in 1982.

For the purposes of this book, however, the focus is on basketball at its highest level, which is the NBA. The best of the best college basketball players graduate to the professional ranks, and there produce the greatest moments in the history of the sport.

Wilt Scores 100

In 1962, the NBA was a fledgling professional league. It was less popular than its college counterpart and far less so than baseball and football. That is why when the last-place New York Knicks played the Philadelphia Warriors in Hershey, Pennsylvania, on March 2, no New York press members were in attendance. Even the presence of Philadelphia superstar Wilt Chamberlain couldn't fill the building.

The 4,000 fans that were there saw history. Chamberlain already had broken the single-game scoring record earlier that season, and that night, he did it again in dramatic fashion. He had 69 points at the end of three quarters, and the announcer began announcing his point total with each basket to fire up the crowd. Wilt the Stilt put up 100 points in a 169-147 win. He also still holds records for free throws made, field goals made, and field goals attempted, all set in that one magnificent game.

Havlicek's Steal

In the 1965 Eastern Conference Finals, the Boston Celtics faced Philadelphia, and the series had reached a seventh and deciding game. The game came down to the wire with Boston leading 110-109 and just five seconds on the clock. Philadelphia was taking the ball out of bounds under their own basket, hoping to set up a desperation shot to get the win. They never got the chance.

Philadelphia's Hal Greer tried to get the ball to teammate Chet Walker but failed to notice a lurking John Havlicek, who stepped into the passing lane and stole Greer's pass by tipping it to the Celtics' Sam Jones. Jones dribbled out the last few seconds to seal the win and the series. The Celtics went on to win the championship over the Lakers in five games.

Reed Plays Hurt

In 1970, the Lakers were back in the finals, this time led by Chamberlain, who was traded there from Philadelphia two seasons earlier. The Lakers had lost the 1969 finals to the Celtics and were looking for redemption. They faced the New York Knicks, led by their own star big man in Willis Reed. In game five, with the series tied at 2-2, Reed tore a muscle in his right leg. The Knicks held on to win that game, but Reed missed game six, which allowed Chamberlain to score 45 in a Laker win.

During warm-ups for game seven in New York, Reed shocked everyone when he took to the floor, bringing the crowd to its feet. He then whipped the fans into a frenzy by scoring the game's first two baskets. The Knicks never looked back, winning 113-99. The opening points were the only ones for Reed in the game.

Magic Starts at Center

Ten years later, a new crop of Lakers was once again in the finals, this time led by the next great franchise big man, Kareem Abdul-Jabbar. In his fifth season in L.A., Abdul-Jabbar had the Lakers in the finals for the first time since he arrived. The biggest difference that season was the addition of rookie sensation point guard Earvin "Magic" Johnson, the Lakers' first overall draft pick.

With the series against Philadelphia tied at 2-2, Abdul-Jabbar badly sprained his ankle in the Lakers' game five win. With Abdul-Jabbar out for game six, Laker coach Paul Westhead turned to his 6'9" (2.1 m) rookie point guard to start at center in his place. The results were pure Magic. Johnson scored 42 points, at one point or another during the game playing all five positions. Johnson also added 15 rebounds and seven assists in the 123-107 win. Johnson became the only rookie in league history to be named the finals' most valuable player (MVP).

GREATEST MOMENTS

Bird Robs Detroit

Johnson had a stellar rookie season in 1980, but he did not win Rookie of the Year to go along with his finals MVP trophy. That honor went to his nemesis, Larry Bird of the Celtics. Bird's Indiana State team lost to Johnson's Michigan State Spartans the year before in the 1979 NCAA Championship Game. The two superstars would meet in the finals for the third time in 1987, but first, the Celtics had to get past a tough Detroit Pistons team in the Eastern Conference Finals.

In a seven-game series with every game won by the home team, the critical moment came in game five in Boston. Down by a point with just five seconds left, the Celtics were defending an inbounds pass by Detroit's Isiah Thomas deep in the Detroit end of the court. Out of nowhere, Bird stole the pass and threw the ball to a streaking Dennis Johnson, who put in the winning layup with a second left on the clock.

Magic's Baby Hook

Bird and the Celtics advanced to play Johnson and the Lakers in the 1987 NBA Finals. The Lakers had now made the finals in six of Johnson's first eight seasons and were known around the league as Showtime. The Lakers had won three of those first five appearances, including going 1-1 against the Celtics.

In game four of the series, the Lakers were leading two games to one but trailing in the game 106-105 with seven seconds left. The Lakers took the ball out of bounds under the Boston basket. Johnson caught the inbounds pass near the left sideline. Johnson beat defender Kevin McHale off the dribble, drove, pulled up, and did his best Abdul-Jabbar impression, throwing up a little hook shot that sailed just over the McHale's fingertips into the basket. The Lakers won 107-106 on a little bit of last-second magic and went on to win the series in six.

GREATEST MOMENTS

Jordan Hits "The Shot"

While Johnson and Bird were dominating the 1980s, Michael Jordan was waiting in the wings. He had been in the league since 1984, but his Chicago Bulls teams had losing records until the 1987-1988 season. In 1988-1989, Jordan led the Bulls to the playoffs again, hoping to improve on a career 5-17 playoff record.

The Bulls faced the favored Cleveland Cavaliers in the first round of the 1989 NBA playoffs. They entered game five in Cleveland, Ohio, leading the series three games to one. The game was tight throughout. Jordan and Cavaliers' guard Craig Ehlo traded baskets three seconds apart to give Cleveland a 100-99 lead with three seconds to go in the fourth quarter. Following a Chicago timeout, Ehlo was covering Jordan when Jordan got free to take the inbounds pass. He took two left-handed dribbles with Ehlo on his right hip and then pulled up at the foul line to hit the series-winning jumper over an outstretched Ehlo at the buzzer.

Jordan Beats the Jazz

By the time the 1998 NBA playoffs rolled around, Jordan had established himself as a prolific playoff performer. He was already a five-time NBA champion and five-time finals MVP as they took on the Utah Jazz in the 1998 finals.

The series went to game six with the Bulls leading three games to two. The Jazz led by a point with less than 30 seconds to go. Jazz forward Karl Malone had the ball in the Bulls' end when Jordan stripped him from behind and dribbled to the top of the Jazz's key. Jazz guard Bryon Russell picked him up as he came over the half court line. Jordan drove inside the three-point line and executed a quick crossover. During the move, he put his left hand on Russell's right hip. To this day, Jazz fans say it should have been a foul, but instead, Jordan pulled up for a 20-footer to give the Bulls an 87-86 lead with five seconds to go. Jordan's clutch shot proved to be the series winner, giving the Bulls their sixth title.

Statue of James Naismith on the campus of Springfield College.

Words to Understand:

calisthenics: the art, practice, or a session of a set of exercises

spectators: people who look on or watch, onlookers, or observers

free throws: unimpeded shots at the basket from the free-throw line, given for a technical fault (one free shot) or a foul (two free shots)

CHAPTER

NAISMITH BALL

Baseball may be America's pastime, and football is the country's most popular sport, but neither game is as uniquely American as basketball. Basketball does not come from other games. It did not evolve, but rather, it was invented.

NAISMITH'S CREATION

The famous saying tells us that necessity is the mother of invention. In the case of basketball, however, motherhood belongs to boredom instead. At the International YMCA Training School in Springfield, Massachusetts, a winter of being confined to indoor activities had left physical education students tired of the usual **calisthenics** and gymnastics. The director of the school tasked one of the part-time instructors to come up with something to inspire the students.

Using two peach baskets, two nails, a hammer, a ladder, and a soccer ball, James Naismith invented basketball. The baskets were nailed to walls on opposite side of the gym, each about 10 feet (3 m) off the floor. Players, nine per side at the time, attempted to score points by throwing the ball into the opponent's basket.

Illustration of Dr. James Naismith's Original 13 Rules of Basketball.

BASKETBALL IS BORN

The game was an instant success. Despite its disorganized and often rough play, the students loved it and were lining up outside the YMCA to play it within two weeks.

When these students returned home, they took the game with them to YMCAs across the country. Staff from Naismith's school were recruited to teach the game in New England. Naismith wrote an article describing the game and its rules, which was published nationally. He had to come up with a name for the sport. One of his student's suggested Naismith Ball, but when the modest Naismith rejected this, the student, Frank Mahan, came up with basketball, which became the clear choice.

EARLY ADJUSTMENTS

Basketball's rules were somewhat fluid at its inception. The number of players required per team was undetermined and would range up to 40 per side for some games. Naismith tended to support his original nine-per-team idea, but by 1900, most games consisted of three 20-minute periods featuring teams of five.

The size of playing areas also varied. Since there were no structures that had been built to accommodate basketball specifically, games were held in venues from armories to skating rinks. Some of these venues had support posts in the middle of the playing area, which savvy players learned to use to pick defenders, a play that still exists today with live players acting as the post.

The standard-size ball and basket were adopted in 1895. The ball was slightly larger than a soccer ball and was held together with thick leather laces that were not very durable. The laces also made the ball's surface uneven, making it hard to handle and difficult to predict.

FINE-TUNING

Spectators began to be commonplace at games around the turn of the century. In some venues, the configuration was such that baskets were affixed to the balcony where spectators were sitting, and they could reach down and interfere with the ball at the basket. Therefore, wire backboards were constructed in these venues to prevent this interference. The wire was soft, however, and would quickly become so dented that it created erratic, unpredictable rebounds. This led to the wire boards being replaced by wooden ones, which were soon adopted in many venues, although some still used a basket hung from the top of a pole.

The first basketball court: Springfield College.

By the mid-1890s, the standard 18-inch (46-cm) iron hoop with a cord net had been created by a Rhode Island company. The nets came with a long cord, and after every basket, the referee would have to pull the cord to lift the net over the hoop, releasing the ball.

Instead of taking the ball out of bounds after baskets, teams would have a jump ball to determine possession every time a basket was scored, a rule that lasted until 1937, when the current rule of giving up possession with a scored basket was enacted.

The rule that gives fouled players **free throws** is also one that evolved over the years. Originally, players who committed fouls were sent to a penalty box, a practice that came from ice hockey. If a team committed three consecutive fouls, their opponents were awarded a single point, the value of a single field goal at the time.

STRATEGY AND STRUCTURE

As the game grew and spread, its structure became more defined. Field goals became worth two points rather than one. The shooting team could designate free throw shooters until 1910 when many leagues adopted the rule that the fouled player was required to take the free throws.

In early basketball games, a team that scored 20 points or more was almost guaranteed to win. Strategy at the time called for a slow-paced game designed to prevent opponents from scoring rather than emphasizing scoring itself. Games were physical with constant fouling. The play itself bore little resemblance to modern-day basketball. Players did not jump while shooting, taking two-handed set shots instead. They also commonly dribbled with both hands at the same time. That was if they dribbled at all, which was not required. In fact, if players did choose to dribble, they were then prohibited from shooting and would have to pass the ball. If that pass should happen to go out of bounds, possession was determined by a wild and dangerous scramble for the errant ball, going to the first team to retrieve it.

PRO HOOPS

Professional basketball's pioneers emerged in the late 1800s, and they did not command quite the enormous salaries that their modern-day counterparts do. Members of the first known pro team in Trenton, New Jersey, made $15 a season. Their first professional game came against a team from Brooklyn, New York, on November 7, 1896, a 16-1 victory.

The venue for that first-ever pro game had a 12-foot (3.7-m) fence around the court, which kept the ball and the players from going into the crowd of about 700 spectators. The fencing meant fewer fights for the ball and greatly increased the pace of games, which led to its adoption by several courts.

PROFESSIONAL LEAGUES FORM

At the turn of the century, there were several pro teams in the Northeast, and these teams began to organize their competition. Teams in the Philadelphia and southern New Jersey area formed the first league in 1898, called the National Basketball League. Teams played a 20-game season schedule, and players made a total of $37.50. The team from Trenton won the inaugural championship.

Other local leagues also formed, but many teams remained independent. The greatest of these at the turn of the century was the Buffalo Germans. The original Germans were a bunch of 14-year-olds from the local YMCA. From 1895 to 1915, they won 792 of 878 games, including a streak of 111 wins in a row. At one point, they were so good that they could command a $5,000 fee for a three-game series.

The Buffalo Germans in 1903.

THE ORIGINAL CELTICS

Another dominant team of the era also hailed from the state of New York. The original Celtics came out of New York City in the 1920s. The Celtics featured players like Horse Haggerty, Johnny Beckman, and Nat Holman. In a two-year stretch from 1922 to 1923, they posted a record of 193-11, attracting huge crowds and big salaries. The Celtics were unique in that they were highly structured in their approach to the game, implementing give-and-go plays, defensive switching, and quick passing to create then find the open man.

When the American Basketball League (ABL) formed in 1925, it invited the Celtics to join, wanting to capture the popularity of a team that averaged 120 wins per 150-game

SPORT KINGS GUM

NAT HOLMAN

season. The Celtics resisted for one season, but joined in 1926, and easily won the league championship. Including the Celtics, however, turned out to be a bad decision on the part of the ABL. Fans disliked the Celtics' rough brand of play and were bored by the team's total dominance. The league tried to curb the rough play by instituting a rule disqualifying players who picked up five fouls, but the league continued to falter and folded in 1931.

NEW YORK RENAISSANCE

Independent teams continued to be strong following the demise of the ABL. From 1932 to 1936, an all-black team from New York was one of the best in the country. The Renaissance, or Rens for short, won 473 of 522 games over that stretch, including 88 in a row. Led by players like Clarence "Fats" Jenkins, Eyre Saitch, and Charles "Tarzan" Cooper, the Rens won the 1939 World Professional Basketball Championship. Being all black, however, the Rens could not join white leagues and, in some states, could not even compete against white teams. In some cities, they would drive in for the game and leave immediately after because they could not find a hotel that accepted blacks.

HARLEM GLOBETROTTERS

When modern-day fans consider all-black teams from New York, they likely first think of the Harlem Globetrotters. Abe Saperstein formed the Globetrotters in 1927 with the philosophy that basketball should entertain. They followed the Rens' world championship win with one of their own in 1940. The Globetrotters lived up to their name, playing all over the world. Combining fast-paced play with expert ball handling and a theatrical flair, they attracted huge crowds, including one of 75,000 in Berlin in 1951. Over the years, they developed several tricks, like players throwing passes that would bounce back to them or rolling the ball from fingertip to fingertip across the shoulders.

The Globetrotters eventually evolved into the all-exhibition comedy and trick-play act that we know today. Independent teams like the Rens and Celtics faded away, but all had a lasting effect on the sport by introducing the elements of pace, ball handling, and showmanship to the professional game.

The Harlem Globetrotters appearing in a 1969 TV comedy special.

Text-Dependent Questions:

1. Who invented basketball and why?

2. By the mid-1890s, the standard 18-inch (46-cm) iron hoop with a cord net had been created by a Rhode Island company. What was the key element of this new net that allowed the referee to release the ball after it was in the hoop?

3. The National Basketball League was formed in 1898 by which two teams?

Research Project:

Create a digital presentation showing how the equipment, court, uniforms, rules, and venues have changed since the inception of basketball.

George Mikan

Words to Understand:

emulated: tried to equal or excel, also imitated with effort to equal or surpass

mantle: an important role or responsibility that passes from one person to another

rookie: an athlete playing his or her first season as a member of a professional sports team

CHAPTER 3

SIZE MATTERS

Back in the 1940s, one of the key elements of modern-day basketball had yet to be introduced, that being the element of height. Tall and athletic were two adjectives that were very rarely used to describe the same person. That was certainly true of a young George Mikan.

THE FIRST BIG MAN

Mikan was 6'10" (2.1 m) by the age of 18, but he was awkward, uncoordinated, and clumsy. He also was determined, however, and despite being unable to make his high school basketball team in Joliet, Illinois, Mikan tried out for the team when he enrolled at DePaul University in 1942.

DePaul coach Ray Meyer saw Mikan's work ethic as he trained relentlessly to improve his skills and decided to give him a chance. By his sophomore year, Mikan was an All-American. He could execute hook shots with either hand and played with confidence. He was named an All-American in his junior and senior years as well.

MIKAN'S LEGACY

Mikan signed with nearby Chicago of the National Basketball League (NBL) for $212,000 after graduation. The Gears built the team around him as Mikan dominated games on both ends of the floor. He was adept at passing the ball out of double teams, and when left in single coverage, he buried hook shot after hook shot. Most players of the era were of average height, and with his considerable height advantage, Mikan was also a superior offensive rebounder. He is the reason leagues went to a 12-foot (3.7-m) rather than a six-foot 1.8-m) lane.

Mikan led the Gears to the NBL title in 1947, averaging 16.5 points and 19.7 rebounds per game. Gears games filled not only the arena in Chicago but buildings around the league as well. That was not enough, however, to prevent the Gears from folding after the 1947 season, and Mikan moved to the Minneapolis Lakers.

THE NBA IS BORN

In 1946, a rival league emerged calling itself the Basketball Association of America. Among its original teams were the New York Knickerbockers, Boston Celtics, Philadelphia Warriors (now in San Francisco as Golden State), and Chicago Stags (now defunct). 1949, the NBL merged with the Basketball Association of America to form the National Basketball Association.

Fans continued to pack the stands to watch Mikan play. He led the NBA in scoring in the league's first three seasons, and the Lakers won three of the first four championships. He retired due to bad knees in 1954 (a comeback attempt in 1956 lasted just 37 games).

THE NEXT GENERATION

Mikan retired for good when Bill Russell was a senior at the University of San Francisco (USF), Russell, also a 6'10" (2.1 m) center, considered Mikan to be his hero, and he **emulated** his game, especially on defense. He led the Dons to two NCAA titles, and at one point his teams won 55 straight games.

Russell went from USF to the Celtics in 1956, and the **rookie** led them to the NBA title game in his first year under the leadership of coach Red Auerbach. Auerbach's Celtics were among the best teams in NBA history, led by Russell on defense, Bob Cousy in transition, and Bill Sharman and Tom Heinsohn on offense. The Celtics lost the championship to St. Louis in double overtime, but Russell had 32 rebounds, and he would go on to be one of the most dominant rebounders in the history of the game.

WILT THE STILT

The Celtics eventually would go on to win nine titles under Auerbach and another two after Russell took over as coach when Auerbach moved to general manager in 1967. At the end of this run, however, Russell was no longer the game's dominant big man. That **mantle** had shifted and belonged to Wilt Chamberlain. Wilt the Stilt came out of Philadelphia in

Wilt Chamberlain

1954 as a 7'2" (2.2 m) high school phenom pursued by practically every university in the country. Chamberlain went to the University of Kansas and promptly scored 52 points in his very first game.

He signed his first NBA contract with the Philadelphia Warriors in 1959 and averaged more than 38 points and 27 rebounds in his rookie season. Three years later, Chamberlain posted one of the greatest offensive seasons in league history, averaging 50 points a game, including nights of 78 points and a record 100 points in a win against the Knicks.

As great as Chamberlain was, he could not will his Philadelphia team past its nemesis, the Celtics. Chamberlain lost to Russell and the Celtics in the playoffs three times from 1962 to 1966. The Warriors moved to the San Francisco Bay area in 1962, and Chamberlain was dealt back to Philadelphia and the expansion 76ers in 1964. He got his revenge on both the Celtics and Warriors in 1967, beating the Russell-less Celtics in the playoffs and the Warriors in the finals. He won a second championship playing for the Lakers in 1972 and retired having scored more than 30,000 points and having grabbed nearly 24,000 rebounds.

New York Knicks vs. Washington Wizards

Text-Dependent Questions:

1. George Mikan, known as the first big man, signed with Chicago of the National Basketball League (NBL) for how much money after graduation?

2. In 1949, which two leagues merged to create the NBA?

3. What is Wilt Chamberlain's nickname?

Research Project:

Make a chart or graph to record the size of players across the ages and their success as well as popularity. In your opinion does size matter in basketball? Explain using the data you collected as evidence of your theory.

College basketball games, like this one between DePaul and LIU in the 1940s, were very different from NBA games, especially after significant rule changes in 1954.

Words to Understand:

beneficiaries: people or groups that receive benefits, profits, or advantages

abundant: present in great quantity, more than adequate

infusion: the addition of something that is needed or helpful

CHAPTER

FREE THROWS AND FAST BREAKS

The advent of the big man certainly changed the professional game in very significant ways, but it was not the most impactful change of the era. In the mid-1950s, games were nonstop physical battles in the lane, with constant pushing, shoving, and fouling. Teams were shooting upwards of 30 free throws a night, and it was a painful ordeal for fans to watch. In addition, teams were employing the strategy of dribbling out the clock when they had a fourth-quarter lead. Changes had to be made.

FIVE FOULS AND 24 SECONDS

In 1954, the league implemented a rule that automatically granted teams a bonus free throw for every opponent foul beginning with the sixth foul committed, whether in the act of shooting or not. The NBA also instituted a 24-second shot clock, requiring teams to attempt a shot before that clock expired. These new rules served to both improve the flow and pace of games as well as increase the total number of possessions. In the 1954-1955 season, scoring increased by a whopping 13.5 points per game over the previous season.

The new rules were a boon to the league's skill players and therefore to the fans as well. With stars like Bob Cousy now able to run the floor without being mugged, fast breaks abounded, and the Celtics were the biggest **beneficiaries**, given their high skill level. They averaged a league-leading 101.5 points per game in 1954-1955 on a foundation of defense, speed, and fast breaks.

SPEED IS NOT ENOUGH

Cousy's ball wizardry and Chamberlain's offensive fireworks were certainly among the elements that kept the game interesting for sports fans during the winter months, but overall, the NBA brand of basketball was considered to be underwhelming as a sport, especially compared to baseball and football.

In 1967, the newly formed American Basketball Association (ABA) sought to raise the excitement level for fans during the winter months. The ABA had no TV deal, but the owners had deep enough pockets to lure some of the NBA's top players. The Warriors' Rick Barry, the NBA's leading scorer, was the first star to sign with the new league. They also signed top players out of college as well, and by 1970, the NBA had a serious fight on its hands.

Bob Cousy

ABOVE THE RIM

The ABA offered fans a different, flashier brand of basketball. It used a colorful red, white, and blue ball. It adopted the three-point shot that was introduced by the defunct American Basketball League, which lasted a short two seasons (1961-1963). The style of play was flamboyant —speedy guards ran the floor with abandon, and the game moved up and down the floor at a high pace. Perhaps most importantly of all, however, slam dunks were encouraged, not frowned upon as they were in the NBA.

The dunk was popularized in the college game by Oklahoma A&M's Bob Kurland during the team's championship run in 1945. The move was seen as a hot dog play by many traditionalists, however, and the NCAA actually banned it from 1967 to 1976.

Dunks were not widely popular in the NBA in the 1960s either but were legal, and some teams did try to capitalize on the thrilling nature of the play. In Baltimore, the Bullets' Gus Johnson was a prolific and powerful dunker who could shatter backboards with his strength. In 1963, the Bullets began playing the sound of a gunshot over the speaker system whenever Johnson slammed one through.

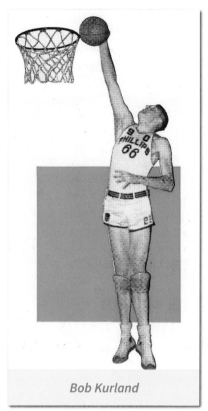

Bob Kurland

DOCTOR J

The Bullets were the exception, however, and while the NBA generally discouraged dunking, the ABA highlighted the play wherever it could. The player who made those opportunities most **abundant** was Julius "Doctor J" Erving. Erving left the University of Massachusetts after his sophomore season to sign with the ABA's Virginia Squires. He played the game like no other player before him. His athleticism and leaping ability were unprecedented. His drives to the rim and ability to control his body in the air resulted in spectacular dunks that regularly brought fans out of their seats.

The 1976 ABA All-Star Game was televised nationally, as was the slam dunk contest preceding it. For his entry in the contest, Erving ran the length of the floor, planted a foot before the foul line and took off. He sailed toward the rim and slammed it through to the delight and disbelief of all watching.

THE LEAGUES BATTLE

Erving gave the ABA the kind of legitimacy it needed to attract other stars like George Gervin, Moses Malone, and David Thompson. One thing the ABA failed to attract was a major TV deal. The league was $50 million in the red by 1976, losing about $5 million a season.

Prior to the 1977 season, the ABA and NBA agreed to terms on a merger. Only four ABA teams survived: the Denver Nuggets, Indiana Pacers, New Jersey Nets, and San Antonio Spurs. Each of the four teams had to pay the NBA an entrance fee, and to raise the funds, the Nets sold Erving to the Philadelphia 76ers for $3 million.

NEW BLOOD

That first season post-merger illustrated vividly not only the skill level of the ABA players but the success the former league's up-tempo style of play could have. Denver won the Midwest Division. Ten of the 24 players in that year's All-Star Game were old ABA players. Four of that season's top 10 scorers and five starters in the NBA Finals were from the ABA as well.

George Gervin

This **infusion** of energy from star players like Gervin, Malone, and Erving was much needed in a league that was struggling with massive image problems. Rumors of widespread drug use throughout the league were rampant. Ugly incidents on the court were tarnishing an already-blemished image. In 1978 alone Kareem Abdul-Jabbar was injured in an on-court brawl; Kermit Washington nearly killed Rudy Tomjanovich in a fight; and superstar center Bill Walton of defending champion Portland broke his foot and missed a third of the season. TV ratings sank as fans quit attending and watching a league whose players were branded as violent drug addicts.

The NBA needed another transfusion, and in 1979, it got a double dose of new blood that changed the league forever.

Text-Dependent Questions:

1. What kind of shot was popularized in a college game by Oklahoma A&M's Bob Kurland in 1945 but banned by the NCAA from 1967 to 1976?

2. What is player Julius Erving's nickname?

3. In the late 1970s the ABA was attracting star players to the league such as George Gervin, Moses Malone, and David Thompson, but what was the one thing the ABA failed to attract?

Research Project:

Go online to find videos of some of the most memorable and important dunks throughout the history of basketball. Use them to create your own mini movie of the greatest dunks of all time. Find out what the NCAA gave as a reason for banning them from play for nine years, and share your thoughts on the role of dunks in today's game.

Former Indiana State basketball star Larry Bird, right, holds up his new Boston Celtics uniform jersey bearing number 33 with Celtics president Red Auerbach, left, at a news conference in Boston, Mass., 1979.

![icon] **Words to Understand:**

layup: a shot made from near the basket, usually by playing the ball off the backboard

charismatic: having great charm or appeal, filled with charisma

apex: climax, peak

CHAPTER

BIRD, MAGIC, AND MICHAEL

The 1979 NCAA Tournament final game was a matchup between Earvin "Magic" Johnson's Michigan State Spartans and Larry Bird's Indiana State Sycamores. Johnson and Bird were drafted into the NBA by iconic franchises that summer, Bird to the Celtics and Johnson to the Los Angeles Lakers. It was exactly what the NBA needed.

THE MAGIC TOUCH

Either the Celtics or the Lakers won eight of the next 10 NBA titles, five for Johnson's Lakers and three for Bird's Celtics. They faced each other in the finals three times, with Johnson getting the upper hand in two of the three, just like in the NCAA final.

Despite being 6'9" (2.1 m), Johnson was the best point guard in the league. Although he could score and rebound like a big man, he dominated games with his passing, making the triple double (10 or more points, rebounds, and assists in a game) commonplace. Because of Johnson, the Lakers had the most feared fast break of the 1980s. With Johnson running the floor, the defense would have to respect the drive to the basket as well as the pull-up jumper and, in doing so, was often burned by the no-look pass to the open man for the easy bucket.

SHOWTIME

Johnson joined a team led by Kareem Abdul-Jabbar, the 7'2" (2.2 m) center who was one of the very few true stars in the league at the time. Abdul-Jabbar was a dominant force on both ends of the floor, scoring and passing on offense and rebounding and blocking shots on defense. His patented sky hook shot had such a high release point that it was unblockable, and Abdul-Jabbar could launch it with either hand.

Kareem Abdul-Jabbar

Those Laker teams of the 1980s also included James Worthy, Michael Cooper, and Kurt Rambis. The teams were dubbed "Showtime" because of the flashy and dynamic style of play they employed. But there was no Showtime without Magic, as he demonstrated in the 1980 NBA Finals against Seattle. Abdul-Jabbar had injured his ankle in a game five win to give the Lakers a 3-2 series lead. Rookie point guard Johnson was tasked with replacing him at center for game six. Johnson scored 42 and chipped in with 15 rebounds to win the Lakers the title.

LARRY LEGEND

In Boston, Bird also found himself surrounded by outstanding teammates. Danny Ainge, Dennis Johnson, Kevin McHale, and Robert Parrish were all first-class players. But as it was with Johnson and the Lakers, Bird was the straw that stirred the drink.

Bird was one of the best shooters in the game. He worked tirelessly at and after every practice on improving his already deadly shot. He revived the below-the-rim skill of shooting the basketball. The NBA had turned into a drive-and-dunk league. He reminded observers of the great Jerry West, another pinpoint jump shooter.

Larry Bird

Bird's skills were on display during the 1987 Eastern Conference Finals against Detroit. In game five, the series was tied 2-2, and the Celtics trailed by a point with just five seconds to play. Detroit just had to inbound the ball to secure the win. Detroit's Isiah Thomas set up to inbound but must have misjudged Bird's quickness because when he threw the ball in, Bird spun off his man and stole the pass, getting it quickly to a wide-open Dennis Johnson for the winning **layup**.

A GREAT SPORTS RIVALRY

The competition between the Celtics and the Lakers for league supremacy was exactly the shot in the arm the NBA needed. When Magic and Bird retired in 1991 and 1992 due to illness and injury, respectively, they left behind a league that was healthy and thriving.

The Bird–Magic rivalry had led to improved TV ratings, and led by these two superstars, the league had cleaned up its act through the 1980s. Average attendance improved 37 percent from 1980 to 1989, reaching the highest level it had ever been. Sponsors came back, and the NBA image had improved dramatically, just in time for the next superstar to launch it into the stratosphere.

A SUPERSTAR EMERGES

Michael Jordan joined the Chicago Bulls after being drafted in 1984. Like the rest of the league, he watched the Celtics dominate the Eastern Conference for most of the 1980s and then watched Thomas and the Pistons win back-to-back titles in 1989 and 1990.

After struggling to find their footing in his first several seasons, the Bulls were becoming a force in the East by the late 1980s, as the Celtics faded. Jordan was league MVP in 1988 and the NBA's leading scorer for six straight seasons when, in 1991, he led the Bulls to the first of three straight titles.

Jordan and the Bulls would win six titles in all in the 1990s, and the **charismatic** Jordan was a marketer's dream. "Be Like Mike" the ad campaign urged, and millions of kids around the country and the world wanted to. His low socks and knee-length shorts look soon became the standard, and emergency rooms around the country were inundated with kids who had bitten their tongues trying to emulate his trademark tongue-wagging style while driving the lane.

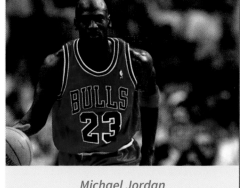

Michael Jordan

Jordan took a season and a half off from basketball after the murder of his father to pursue an unsuccessful attempt at pro baseball. When he returned, he was more focused than ever. In 1995-1996, his Bulls won 72 games and a fourth title. Jordan was at his acrobatic best, even at 33.

His legacy was in no need of cementing by the time the 1997 finals found Jordan and the Bulls tied 2-2 with Utah. In game five, Jordan was suffering from the flu and was feverish and dehydrated throughout the game. Despite his condition, the Bulls looked to Jordan at the end of the game with the score tied at 87. He found the energy to drain one final three-point shot that held up as the game-winner. The Bulls won the next game to repeat as champions.

Jordan, Johnson, and Bird were actually all teammates at one time on the 1992 U.S. Olympic basketball team. The team has been called the greatest collection of talent ever, in any sport, and was dubbed the "Dream Team." They won the gold medal by an average margin of 44 points per game. The team also included Hall of Famers Charles Barkley, Clyde Drexler, Patrick Ewing, David Robinson, Scottie Pippen, Karl Malone, and John Stockton.

WOMEN IN BASKETBALL

The U.S. women's team finished in the bronze medal position at those 1992 Games. This finish was sandwiched between gold medal results in the 1988 and 1996 Games. American women have won gold at seven Olympic Games since the women's game became a medal sport in 1976 (it had been a demonstration sport since 1924). The United States has medaled in every Games it has entered.

1996 Atlanta Olympic Games, Gold Medal

Women's basketball developed in colleges across the country, from that first game in 1896 to the first NCAA Women's Tournament in 1982. Two of the coaches who advanced the modern game are Pat Summitt and Geno Auriemma.

Summitt was the longtime coach of women's basketball at the University of Tennessee. Between 1974 and 2012, her Volunteers teams won eight NCAA titles. Her 1,098 wins are the most ever by any college basketball coach (Duke University men's coach Mike Krzyzewski is not far behind). She is the only woman on the *Sporting News* list of 50 Greatest Coaches of All Time. Summitt is also a Presidential Medal of Freedom recipient.

Auriemma is the only women's coach with more titles than Summitt, having guided the University of Connecticut program to 10 championships. Only UCLA's legendary John Wooden has as many. Like Summitt, he is a seven-time Coach of the Year winner. He also coached the women's team to gold medals at the 2000 and 2012 Olympic Games.

Outside of college and the Olympics, women also play professionally in the Women's National Basketball Association (WNBA). The WNBA is a wholly owned subsidiary of the NBA, and their NBA counterparts financially support the 12 teams. The league is, therefore, able to operate regardless of low revenue (only half the teams were profitable in 2014), lagging attendance (2012 to 2014 are three of the league's four lowest average attendance seasons), and low TV ratings (less than 250,000 viewers per game).

Pat Summitt

JORDAN'S LEGACY

The WNBA was launched in 1997 with the game at its **apex**. Truly, the WNBA is actually part of Michael Jordan's legacy. In the 1990s, Jordan was the most recognized athlete on the planet, and he gave the NBA and basketball itself a profile like it had never had before. The sport he handed off to the superstars of today when he retired in 2003 was in better shape than ever before.

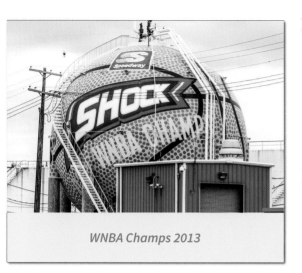

WNBA Champs 2013

Text-Dependent Questions:

1. The Lakers had the most feared fast break of the 1980s because of which player?

2. A rivalry in the 1980s between which two players led to improved TV ratings and the highest attendance levels at games there had ever been?

3. American women have won gold at how many Olympic Games since the women's game became a medal sport in 1976?

Research Project:

Design a questionnaire to interview coaches, players, administrators, and fans about how people rate their own commitment to the team in relation to its success. For example, do fans remain fans when their team is losing?

DeMarcus Cousins

Words to Understand:

touted: described or advertised boastfully, publicized or praised extravagantly

parallels: having the same direction, course, nature, or tendency

field goal: a successful shot worth two points—three points if shot from behind the three-point line

CHAPTER 6

MODERN-DAY STARS

Basketball is a team sport, but such is the structure of the game that a single dominant player can easily control it. More so than the other team sports, basketball's greatest stars command the spotlight when they step on the court.

THE BIG MEN

DeMarcus Cousins played only one year at the University of Kentucky before declaring himself ready for the NBA. The Sacramento Kings agreed, selecting the 6'11" (2.1 m) Cousins with the fifth pick in the 2010 draft.

Cousins quickly established himself as a dominant low-post player. His early career, however, was marred by issues on and off the court, leading to suspensions and a league-leading 16 technical fouls in the 2011-2012 season. By 2015, however, Cousins had matured along with his game. He was named to the NBA All-Star Team for the first time in 2015.

Dwight Howard has been named to the All-Star Team eight times since being drafted first overall by Orlando in 2004. The 6'11" (2.1 m) Howard is the all-time leading scorer in Magic history. He left Orlando for a season with the Lakers in 2012 before joining Houston in 2013.

At 275 lbs. (124.7 kg), Howard is imposing and difficult to defend near the basket. No player in NBA history has reached 9,000 career rebounds faster than Howard. He led the league in total rebounds five seasons in a row, an NBA record. He also led in blocks twice.

Marc Gasol was not nearly as highly touted as Howard when he was drafted out of Europe, going to the Lakers in the second round in 2007. But he rounded into one of the best defenders and top centers in the league.

Gasol never played for the Lakers, who traded his rights to Memphis after the draft in a package that included his brother Pau going to Los Angeles. The seven-footer is a two-time NBA all-star as a member of the Grizzlies. He also was named the NBA Defensive Player of the Year in 2013.

Al Jefferson, 6'10" (2.1 m), was the first-round draft pick of the Boston Celtics in 2004 and has been a force in the middle for three other teams since. Jefferson came off the bench during his first two seasons with the Celtics, finally establishing himself as a starter in his third season, averaging 16 points and 11 rebounds. Boston traded him to Minnesota as part of a package of players to obtain Kevin Garnett. Jefferson has averaged more than 16 points in every season since, including hitting more than 20 points per game three times in his career, twice with Minnesota and once in Charlotte.

Like Jefferson, Andre Drummond was a highly **touted** first-round pick, going to the Pistons in 2012 after one year at the University of Connecticut. Drummond came off the bench during his first season in Detroit but took over as the starter for 2013-2014.

The 6'10" (2.1 m) Drummond is one of the league's dominant offensive rebounders, battling hard on every possession under the opponent's basket. In 2013 and 2014 he led the NBA in both total offensive rebounds and personal fouls.

POST PLAYERS

In the modern NBA, the effective forward needs to be able to catch the ball and score with it in the low post equally as well as they can step back and hit an 18-foot jump shot.

Cleveland's LeBron James is the ultimate example of the player with the full set of skills. The 6'8" (2 m) James went directly from dominating games in high school to doing the same at the NBA level all in the same year.

LeBron James

Kevin Garnett

James can score from the inside or outside as well as almost anyone in the game. He led the league in scoring in 2008 while making more free throws than anyone in the NBA due to his work on the inside. He is also one of the best defenders in the game. James has been named to the NBA All-Defensive Team five times.

Kevin Garnett has a story that **parallels** that of James in many ways. He also was drafted right out of high school in the first round to play with the Minnesota Timberwolves in 1995. Like James, his game is very versatile as he possesses the ability to score from under the basket as well as several feet from it. Garnett, 6'11" (2.1 m), is the 2004 NBA MVP and a four-time rebounding champ.

Dirk Nowitzki　　　　　*Kevin Durant*　　　　　*LaMarcus Aldridge*

Garnett is also an excellent defensive player who was named to the All-Defensive Team nine times. This includes 2008, when he led the Celtics to the NBA Championship.

Dirk Nowitzki is also an NBA champion, winning the title in 2011 over James and the Miami Heat. The German-born seven-footer was the finals MVP that year as the Mavericks triumphed in six games. It was the ultimate team accomplishment for a player with plenty of individual honors.

Nowitzki is a 13-time all-star, including the 2007 season, in which he was named NBA MVP. For his career, he has averaged more than 25 points and 10 rebounds in the playoffs, one of only four players in NBA history to do so.

Playoff success has eluded Kevin Durant in his career. He lost his only trip to the Finals in 2012. On every other front, however, the 6'9" (2 m) forward has exceeded expectations. Those expectations were high as the second overall pick out of the University of Texas in 2007 by Seattle (now Oklahoma City). Durant started by winning Rookie of the Year, averaging more than 20 points per game.

Since then, Durant has been an all-star every season, starting with his third in the league. He also has led the league in scoring four times and was the NBA MVP in 2012.

Like Durant, University of Texas teammate LaMarcus Aldridge was also the second overall pick in the draft, but the year before in 2006. Aldridge played nine seasons with the team that selected him, the Portland Trail Blazers. He signed as a free agent with San Antonio after the 2014-2015 season.

Aldridge, 6'11" (2.1 m), is a four-time NBA all-star. He led the league in **field goal** attempts from within the arc from 2013 to 2015 but also added the three-point shot to his game in 2015. He took nearly as many three-point shots that season (105) as he did in all his previous seasons combined (119).

THE SHOOTERS

When Oklahoma City selected Arizona State's James Harden with the third pick in the 2009 NBA draft, they were looking for a player to complement dynamic star Kevin Durant from the backcourt. But Oklahoma City coach Scott Brooks preferred to use Harden off the bench. Harden was named NBA Sixth Man of the Year in 2012 as the Thunder reached the NBA Finals.

Harden refused to resign with Oklahoma City and was then traded to Houston for the 2012-2013 season. Given the chance to start, he blossomed into a three-time all-star. In 2015, Harden led the league in minutes played, free throws attempted and made, and total points scored.

One of the key main rivals for Harden and the Rockets in the Western Conference is the Golden State Warriors. His counterpart on that team is the Warriors' 2011 first-round draft pick from Washington State, Klay Thompson. Thompson is the son of former first overall pick in 1978 and Laker star Mychal Thompson, who won two championships with L.A. in the 1980s.

Klay Thompson got halfway to his father's championship ring total in 2015, when he helped lead Golden State to the team's first championship in 40 years. The 6'7" (2 m) Thompson was named to the NBA All-Star Team that season, hitting 43.7 percent of his three-point attempts while scoring 21.7 points per game.

Thompson's all-star counterpart from the Eastern Conference in both 2015 and 2016 was Jimmy Butler of Chicago. The Bulls took Butler in the first round of the 2011 draft out of Marquette University.

James Harden

Klay Thompson

Jimmy Butler

The 6'7" (2 m) Butler was also voted the NBA's Most Improved Player in 2015 when he increased his points per game over the previous season from 13.1 to 20.0. He was even better in the playoffs, scoring nearly 23 points per game. In both all-star seasons, Butler led the NBA in minutes played. He is also a two-time NBA All-Defensive Second Team member.

As Butler is becoming the new face of the Bulls franchise, Dwayne Wade has had the same role for the Miami Heat for years. Wade has been there for his team when it counts—in the playoffs. Wade, 6'4" (1.9 m), has played in the NBA Finals five times and has won three championships.

Wade contributes to the success of his teams most prominently on the offensive end. On the playoff run that resulted in the first Heat championship in 2006, he averaged more than 28 points per game. Wade also led the NBA in scoring in 2009.

In 2009, the Toronto Raptors selected DeMar DeRozan from the University of Southern California with the ninth overall pick. He stepped into the Raptors starting lineup a few weeks into his rookie season and did not look back. DeRozan steadily improved his game and, along with it, the postseason chances of the Raptors.

DeRozan had a special year in 2013-2014, making the All-Star Team on the strength of a 22.7 points-per-game average. He has averaged 22.5 points per game in the playoffs.

Dwayne Wade

DeMar DeRozan

THE GENERALS

To execute a game plan, coaches need a player on the floor who knows and understands the objectives of each play and who can read defenses and adjust accordingly. That player, the floor general, is the point guard.

Golden State's Stephen Curry is one of the best floor generals in the game. Drafted seventh overall out of Davidson by the Warriors in 2009, the 6'3" (1.9 m) Curry was the runner-up for Rookie of the Year, averaging more than 17 points and nearly six assists a game.

Curry is a deadly outside shooter. He has three of the top five seasons in total three-point baskets made to his credit, including the top two. He shot 272 in 2013 and then 286 in 2015. In that 2015 season, Curry led the Warriors to their first NBA Championship in 40 years and was named NBA MVP.

UCLA product Russell Westbrook was drafted fourth overall just one year before Curry, by Seattle in 2008. The Seattle franchise moved to Oklahoma City before the 2008-2009 season, and Westbrook played his rookie season for the Thunder.

Beginning with his third season, the four-time all-star has averaged more than 20 points per game every year. This includes the 2014-2015 season, when the 6'3" (1.9 m) Westbrook averaged 28.1 points per game to lead the league in scoring. Westbrook has yet to break through in the playoffs, losing to Miami in the Thunder's only Finals appearance in 2012.

Playoff success has also eluded Chris Paul since he joined the league out of Wake Forest in 2005. He won Rookie of the Year playing for New Orleans, scoring 16.1 points per game.

Stephen Curry

Russell Westbrook

Chris Paul

Paul, however, is a classic pass-first point guard, looking for the open man before he looks for his own shot. Paul, 6'0" (1.8 m), is a four-time NBA assists leader. He is also a tenacious on-ball defender, leading the league in steals six times. CP3, as he is commonly known, has been named to the NBA All-Defensive Team five times. The eight-time all-star, who was traded to the L.A. Clippers in 2011, has never been to the Finals.

Expectations were high for John Wall as the first overall pick out of Kentucky in 2010, and he has not disappointed since the Washington Wizards made him the top choice. In 2014, the 6'4" (1.9 m) Wall recorded more assists than anyone else in the league. That passing prowess got him selected to the All-Star Team. His continued improvement as a shooter is one reason that he also was named to the All-Star Team in 2015 as Wall set career highs in shooting percentage as well as rebounds and assists per game. With world-class speed and athleticism, more all-star appearances are in Wall's future.

Portland's Damian Lillard made his first all-star appearance opposite Wall in 2014. Lillard entered the league with a splash the year before, debuting as the Trail Blazers' starting point guard as a rookie and starting every game. In fact, Lillard played more minutes than any other player in the league, rookie or otherwise, and was named Rookie of the Year.

Lillard's success continued in his third season, where he set career highs in scoring, shooting percentage, steals, and rebounds, and he was again selected to be an all-star. Lillard, 6'3" (1.9 m), also has averaged more than 22 points per game in the playoffs.

John Wall   Damian Lillard

Text-Dependent Questions:

1. Which player has been named to the All-Star Team eight times since being drafted first overall by Orlando in 2004?

2. Who led the league in scoring in 2008 while making more free throws than anyone in the NBA, is also one of the best defenders in the game, and has been named to the NBA All-Defensive Team five times?

3. In the 2015 season, which player led the Warriors to their first NBA Championship in 40 years and was named NBA MVP?

Research Project:

Look up the players taken in the first round of the last 10 entry drafts. Prepare a presentation outlining which of these high picks have been a hit versus which were busts. Define your criteria for determining success (number of games played in the NBA, point production, all-star selections and awards, etc.). Based on the results, rank each team according to their first-round draft success.

SHAQUILLE O'NEAL

CHARLES BARKLEY

LARRY BIRD

KAREEM ABDUL-JABBAR

LEBRON JAMES

TIM DUNCAN

BILL RUSSELL (LEFT)

MICHAEL JORDAN

HAKEEM OLAJUWON

JOHN STOCKTON

BASKETBALL HALL OF FAME

KOBE BRYANT

The Naismith Memorial Basketball Hall of Fame is located in Springfield, Massachusetts. James Naismith invented the game at the Springfield YMCA in 1891. Seventy-seven years later, the Hall opened in 1968. Among the first inductees were Naismith, George Mikan, and Phog Allen. The first class was selected in 1959, nine years before the building itself opened. The current building is more than 40,000 square feet, housing memorials to the careers of nearly 350 members. The basketball Hall is the only one of the four major team sports that elects its members with an anonymous vote.

Scan here to go to the Basketball Hall of Fame website.

CHAPTER 7

BASKETBALL'S GREATEST PLAYERS

Like any sport, the way basketball is played evolved over the years. The game has shifted from being dominated by big men in the 1950s and 1960s to a perimeter game dominated by long-range shooters in the 2010s and beyond.

Throughout this evolution, players of all shapes and sizes have thrived at the professional level. Calvin Murphy at 5'9" (1.8 m) had a Hall of Fame career in the 1970s as a point guard for San Diego and Houston. Despite his lack of size, he was drafted in the second round for his defense, quickness, and superior free throw shooting. Ralph Sampson at 7'4" (2.2 m) made the Hall of Fame with a completely different set of skills. The first overall pick in 1983 was coveted not only for his size but also for his agility under the basket.

Where winning factors into the equation as to which are the sport's greatest players has long been a point of debate. While some players excelled in the clutch moments, pulling out victories when it mattered most, others fell short with championships on the line. But should that negate a career with superior statistical results? Jim Loscutoff and Robert Horry each won seven championships, more than Michael Jordan or Kareem Abdul-Jabbar.

From post players to ball handlers, jump shooters to lane driving specialists, players possessing a wide range of abilities have risen to the very top of the game.

CENTERS

Kareem Abdul-Jabbar entered the NBA as 7'2" (2.2 m) Lew Alcindor after a dominant stint at UCLA. The first overall pick by the Milwaukee Bucks in 1969, Alcindor changed his name to Kareem Abdul-Jabbar after leading the Bucks to the title in 1971.

Abdul-Jabbar won five other titles after going to the L.A. Lakers in 1975. Along with his six championships, he holds the record for all-star selections with 19. Abdul-Jabbar was also a two-time Finals MVP and six-time league MVP. Known for his signature post move, the skyhook, Abdul-Jabbar was a prolific scorer. He retired in 1989 having scored more points than any other player in league history.

Abdul-Jabbar passed Wilt Chamberlain on the career-scoring list during the 1983-1984 season, 11 years after Chamberlain retired from the Lakers. Only Michael Jordan scored more points per game during his career than Wilt the Stilt.

At 7'1" (2.2 m) and nearly 300 lbs. (136 kg), Chamberlain was virtually unguardable in the post during his years with the Warriors, Sixers, and Lakers, leading the league in scoring seven times and in rebounding 11 times. He remains the career rebounding leader in league history, a record that will easily endure beyond 50 years. He won a championship with the Sixers in 1967 and another with the Lakers five seasons later.

The man just behind Chamberlain on the career rebounding list is defensive giant Bill Russell. Russell was a standout for the Boston Celtics from 1956 to 1969. He was an all-star in each of his 12 full seasons and won league MVP five times. The 6'10" (2.1 m) Russell led the Celtics to a record 11 championships, including eight in a row.

Russell was a winner at every level. As an amateur, he was a two-time state champion in high school in Oakland. He also led the University of San Francisco to two NCAA Championships and the U.S. Olympic basketball team to a gold medal in 1956 at Melbourne.

Wilt Chamberlain

Another Olympic gold medal-winning center also known for his defensive prowess was 7'0" (2.1 m) Hakeem Olajuwon. Olajuwon played all but 61 games of his 18-year career with the Houston Rockets. A 12-time all-star, he averaged more than 21 points per game in that time but was better known for changing the game at his end of the floor.

Olajuwon has 3,830 career blocked shots, more than any other player in NBA history. He led the league in blocks three times and in rebounds twice. During the 1990s, Olajuwon led Houston to championships in 1994 and 1995, winning Finals MVP both times. He also played for the U.S. team that won the 1996 Olympic basketball gold medal.

In the 1995 NBA Finals, Olajuwon and the Rockets beat an upstart Orlando Magic team led by a young Shaquille O'Neal. O'Neal was the first overall pick in the draft in 1992 and, in just three short seasons, helped Orlando go from lottery pickers to the Finals. O'Neal eventually would win three straight titles from 2000 to 2002 with the Lakers. He won the fourth title of his 19-year career in 2006 with the Miami Heat.

The 7'1" (2.2 m) O' Neal, better known as Shaq, had his best season in 2000, winning not only the title but also league MVP, finals MVP, and the scoring title. The 15-time all-star ranks in the top 15 in career rebounds, blocks, and points.

Shaq was dominant in his era, like Chamberlain was in his, but only Abdul-Jabbar ranks in the top three in career points (1), rebounds (3), and blocks (3).

Kareem Abdul-Jabbar

Shaquille O'Neal

FORWARDS

When Lebron James retires, he undoubtedly will be at the top end of the list of greatest forwards ever to lace up a pair of sneakers. But will he be number one on the list? Only time will tell if his legacy can rival that of Tim Duncan.

James was a Cleveland-area high school phenom. He was Ohio's Mr. Basketball as a sophomore and National High School Player of the Year as a junior, neither of which had ever been done.

Drafted first overall by the Cleveland Cavaliers right out of high school, the 6'8" (2 m) James won Rookie of the Year in 2003. In 2007, he led Cleveland to the Finals, where Duncan and the Spurs swept them. In 2010, he and Chris Bosh of Toronto were both free agents, and they decided to sign with Miami. They teamed with Dwayne Wade to lead the Heat to four straight Finals appearances, winning two. James is also a four-time NBA MVP and an 11-time all-star.

Duncan, 6'11" (2.1 m), was also the number one pick in the draft, coming out of Wake Forest in 1997. He played his entire career with the San Antonio Spurs, the team he led to five NBA Championships. Duncan is a 15-time all-star and two-time NBA MVP.

Duncan is top 10 in career blocks and rebounds and top 15 in points. His playoff legacy is also impressive. Only four players have more career playoff points than Duncan. He was named finals MVP three times, in 1999, 2003, and 2005. Duncan dominated games on both ends of the floor, excelling when the games mattered most. No one in NBA history has more career playoff point–rebound double-doubles than Duncan.

Before Duncan came along, 6'9" (2.1 m) Larry Bird widely was considered to be the best forward ever to play. Some will say he still holds that distinction. After a stellar career at Indiana State, Bird entered the NBA in 1979 and immediately made an impact on his Boston Celtics team. He led the team to the Conference Finals in the playoffs while winning Rookie of the Year.

Bird's Celtics went on to win three NBA titles in the 1980s. He was named NBA MVP three times and Finals MVP twice. The 12-time all-star is also one of the best free throw shooters in NBA history.

Charles Barkley   LeBron James   Tim Duncan

When it comes to free throw shooting, no one in NBA history has made as many as Karl Malone. In his 19-year career, Malone attempted more than 2,000 free throws more than anyone ever has, and made more than 1,000 more.

The 6'9" (2.1 m) Malone played all but one season with the Utah Jazz and made his living going to the basket off the pick and roll and on fast breaks. He led the league in free throws made seven times. Only Abdul-Jabbar has more career points than Malone. He is a two-time all-star and 14-time MVP. The biggest knock on Malone is that he was never able to win a championship, losing three times in the Finals.

Another one of the game's great power forwards who was never able to win a championship was Charles Barkley. Known as the Round Mound of Rebound, he was dominant in the paint, especially when it came to offensive rebounding. Barkley led the league in offensive rebounds for three consecutive seasons from 1987 to 1989. An 11-time all-star, he was NBA MVP in 1993.

The 6'6" (2 m) Barkley played with the 76ers, the Phoenix Suns, and the Houston Rockets. He went to the Finals with the Suns in 1993, losing to Michael Jordan and the Bulls in six games. It was his only trip to the Finals. Only Barkley, Abdul-Jabbar, Chamberlain, and Malone have more than 20,000 points, 10,000 rebounds, and 4,000 assists in their careers.

SHOOTING GUARDS

The best shooting guard ever to play the game is also the greatest basketball player in history. Some say it was Russell or Abdul-Jabbar, and younger fans will point to the exploits of Kobe Bryant and LeBron James. None of them was Michael Jordan.

Jordan was famously the third pick of the 1983 draft. Future NBA Champion and Hall of Famer Hakeem Olajuwon was the first pick. Portland chose 7'1" (2.2 m) Sam Bowie second, a decision that has often been called the worst draft choice in professional sports history.

Jordan changed the fortunes of the Chicago Bulls and became the face of the NBA, setting new scoring records en route to six NBA titles. The 6'6" (2 m) Jordan took the NBA to new heights on and off the floor. As the Nike ad campaign suggested, everyone wanted to "Be Like Mike." In 2014, 11 years after his retirement, Nike still paid Jordan $90 million. The five-time MVP and 10-time scoring leader holds the record for career points per game in both the regular season and playoffs.

Kobe Bryant could never quite Be Like Mike, but he came close at the peak of his career. The Philadelphia high school sensation became the first high school guard ever to be drafted in the first round when the Lakers traded Vlade Divac to Charlotte to pick him in 1996. The 6'6" (2 m) 17-year-old would become one of the of the league's fiercest competitors, eventually leading the Lakers to five NBA titles.

Michael Jordan

Kobe Bryant

Dwayne Wade

His first three titles were won from 2000 to 2002 alongside Hall of Famer Shaquille O'Neal. The next two were won in 2009 and 2010, with Bryant as the focal point. He was named MVP in both years. The 17-time all-star and 2008 NBA MVP is third on the all-time points list behind Abdul-Jabbar and Malone. Bryant is also top 15 in career steals.

The man who drafted Bryant in 1996 was also a legendary Laker guard. Before Kobe and Magic, there was Jerry West. West, who would go on to become the longtime general manager of the Lakers, was drafted second overall by the Minneapolis Lakers in 1960. West was an all-star in each of his 14 seasons, all with the Lakers.

In his first 10 seasons, the 6'2" (1.9 m) West led the Lakers to the Finals seven times but lost them all, including six to the Celtics. In the 1969 Lakers' seven-game loss to Boston, West was named Finals MVP despite playing for the losing team, the only time this has ever happened. West finally led the Lakers to the NBA Championship in 1972.

Clyde "The Glide" Drexler was another great player who had limited success winning championships. He left the University of Houston in 1983 as a junior after losing in the NCAA Tournament Final Four in consecutive years. His first NBA team was the Portland Trail Blazers. The 6'7" (2 m) Drexler led Portland to two NBA Finals appearances. In 1990, they lost to Detroit, and in 1992 they lost to Chicago. Drexler finally won a title with the Houston Rockets in 1995.

Drexler was known for his extraordinary leaping ability, but he played a full court game. Only he, Oscar Robertson, and John Havlicek have more than 20,000 points, 6,000 rebounds, and 6,000 assists for their careers. He also ranks in the top 10 for career steals.

Dwayne Wade ranks in the top 20 in points per game in a career. That may surprise many fans, given that he played four seasons with LeBron James. The 6'4" (1.9 m) Wade, however, always has displayed a knack for scoring.

The fifth overall pick in 2003 out of Marquette, Wade averaged 21.5 points per game as a first team All-American in his draft year. He played for the Miami Heat, helping the team steadily improve their playoff runs until reaching the Finals in 2006. In the series against Dallas, Wade scored more than 35 points in four straight games to win the title and the MVP award. Wade, an all-star in all but his rookie season, also won titles in 2012 and 2013.

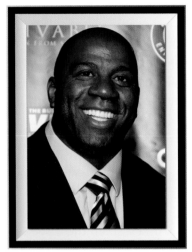

Oscar Robertson   *Magic Johnson*   *Jason Kidd*

POINT GUARDS

The point guard is the quarterback on the court. He calls the shots and sets up the plays. No one gets more touches, and the offense is dictated by his decisions. It is perhaps the most crucial position in the game. As far as point guards go, the choice is just as easy as that at shooting guard. Very few will argue with calling Magic Johnson the greatest point guard ever to play.

After bursting onto the scene with a championship-winning, Rookie of the Year season, Johnson went on to have a spectacular career. A broken foot in his second year is the only reason he was not an all-star in each of his 12 seasons. At 6'9" (2.1 m), Johnson revolutionized the point guard position. At his size, he was a true triple threat to score, pass, or rebound the ball. His 138 triple-doubles are the second most of all time.

Johnson was instrumental in the Lakers winning five championships in the 1980s. He was the NBA Finals MVP in 1980, 1982, and 1987. Johnson led the league in steals twice and in assists four times.

The king of the triple-double was Johnson's boyhood idol, 6'5" (2 m) Oscar Robertson. Coming out of the University of Cincinnati in 1960, "The Big O" was drafted first overall by the Cincinnati Royals (now the Sacramento Kings) and was Rookie of the Year. He was an all-star in each of his first 12 seasons, but only the first 10 were with Cincinnati. The Royals traded Robertson, the 1964 NBA MVP, to Milwaukee in 1970.

In Milwaukee, Robertson teamed with Lew Alcindor (later Kareem Abdul-Jabbar) to make the Bucks a dominant force. Milwaukee won the championship in 1971. He led the league in assists six times and had a record 181 career triple-doubles.

Third on the list of all-time triple-doubles is 6'4" (1.9 m) Jason Kidd. Kidd was the second overall pick out of the University of California, Berkeley, by the Dallas Mavericks in 1995. He won Rookie of the Year that season. Kidd played for four different teams in his 21-year career. Despite being an all-star in 1996, Dallas traded Kidd to Phoenix in 1997, and that's where his game blossomed.

Kidd had 12 all-star seasons, including all of his full seasons in Phoenix. He led the league in assists for three straight years and was considered the best playmaker in the sport. He finally won a championship when he returned to Dallas in 2011 near the end of his career.

A championship eluded John Stockton over the course of his career. The Hall of Famer played his entire 19-year career for the Utah Jazz, making it to the Finals twice, in 1997 and 1998. The Jazz lost both Finals series to Michael Jordan and the Chicago Bulls.

The 6'1" (1.9 m) Stockton had a reputation as a hard-nosed defender and was extremely durable. Arguably the greatest passer ever to play, Stockton led the league in assists nine times. He also led the league in steals twice. The 10-time all-star is the NBA's all-time leader in both steals and assists. Stockton has five of the top six assist seasons in league history.

The other player besides Stockton with one of the all-time top six assist seasons is Isiah Thomas. The 6'1" (1.9 m) Detroit Pistons star was the team's pick at second overall in the 1981 draft. Like Stockton, he played each of his 13 seasons with the same team. Unlike Stockton, he was able to lead the Pistons to two championships, back-to-back wins in 1989 and 1990. He was named MVP in the 1990 Finals victory over Portland, where he averaged more than 20 points and eight assists per game.

Thomas led the NBA in assists in 1984 and 1985. He was an all-star in all but his final injury-plagued season.

Career Snapshots

Centers

#6 BILL RUSSELL 1956-69

15.1 points per game
22.5 rebounds per game
4.3 assists per game

#13 WILT CHAMBERLAIN 1959-73

30.1 points per game
22.9 rebounds per game
4.4 assists per game

#33 KAREEM ABDUL-JABBAR 1969-89

24.6 points per game
11.2 rebounds per game
3.6 assists per game

#34 HAKEEM OLAJUWON 1984-2002

21.8 points per game
11.1 rebounds per game
3.1 blocks per game

#34 SHAQUILLE O'NEAL 199-2011

23.7 points per game
10.9 rebounds per game
2.5 assists per game

All the above athletes are members of the Hall of Fame

Forwards

#33 LARRY BIRD 1979-92

24.3 points per game
10.0 rebounds per game
6.3 assists per game

#34 CHARLES BARKLEY 1984-2000

22.1 points per game
11.7 rebounds per game
3.9 assists per game

#32 KARL MALONE 1985-2004

25 points per game
10.1 rebounds per game
3.6 assists per game

#21 TIM DUNCAN 1997- Present

19.5 points per game
11.0 rebounds per game
3.1 assists per game

#23 LEBRON JAMES 2003- Present

27.3 points per game
7.1 rebounds per game
6.9 assists per game

Shooting Guards

#44 JERRY WEST 1960-74

27 points per game
5.8 rebounds per game
6.7 assists per game

#22 CLYDE DREXLER 1983-98

20.4 points per game
6.1 rebounds per game
5.6 assists per game

#23 MICHAEL JORDAN 1984-2003

30.1 points per game
6.2 rebounds per game
5.3 assists per game

#24 KOBE BRYANT 1996- Present

25.4 points per game
5.3 rebounds per game
4.8 assists per game

#3 DWAYNE WADE 2003- Present

24.1 points per game
4.9 rebounds per game
5.9 assists per game

Point Guards

#14 OSCAR ROBERTSON 1960-74

25.7 points per game
7.5 rebounds per game
9.5 assists per game

#11 ISIAH THOMAS 1981-94

19.2 points per game
3.6 rebounds per game
9.3 assists per game

#32 EARVIN "MAGIC" JOHNSON 1979-96

19.5 points per game
7.2 rebounds per game
11.2 assists per game

#5 JASON KIDD 1984-2000

12.6 points per game
6.3 rebounds per game
8.7 assists per game

#12 JOHN STOCKTON 1984-2003

13.1 points per game
2.7 rebounds per game
10.5 assists per game

Words to Understand:

attribute: a usually good quality or feature that someone or something has

prospects: people or something that are likely to succeed or to be chosen

arc: the three-point line

CHAPTER 8

THE FUTURE OF BASKETBALL

Trends come and go in all aspects of life, and the NBA is no exception. From baggy, knee-length shorts and elbow sleeves to the 24-second shot clock and the three-point line, the game has evolved over the years and will continue to adapt in the future.

STRETCHING UP AT THE POINT

Height always has been an **attribute** in the sport of basketball. The one position where it is not expected or required is at point guard. In Chapter 6, the tallest player listed among the point guards is John Wall at 6'4" (1.9 m). Having ball handlers be lower to the ground has been the prevailing wisdom in the sport for generations.

There have obviously been notable exceptions. Hall of Famers Magic Johnson and Oscar Robertson were 6'9" (2.1 m) and 6'5" (2 m), respectively, but were exceptions to the standard. Now, the sport is trending toward a future with taller players running the point. In the 2015 NBA draft, four of the first seven point guards taken were 6'5" (2 m) or taller. The 2016 recruiting class is trending in a similar direction. Top point guard **prospects** Troy Brown, Kobi Simmons, and Lonzo Ball are all at least 6'5" (2 m). The era of the big ball handler could be upon us soon.

POSITIONLESS BASKETBALL

While point guard size is trending upward, the other four positions are becoming more and more interchangeable. LeBron James, at 6'8" (2 m), can play all five positions. When Golden State won the championship in 2015, they mostly employed a lineup where no player was taller than 6'8" (2 m). The lack of talented big men in the vein of Hakeem Olajuwon or Shaquille O'Neal has led teams to prioritize skilled, athletic, mid-sized players who can run the floor, defend, and shoot.

The Phoenix Suns had some success with this sort of lineup under Coach Mike D'Antoni in the mid-2000s with point guard Steve Nash and a cast of relatively small supporting players. Steve Kerr was the general manager of those Phoenix teams, and he was the coach of Golden State as well. With the Warriors winning the title with a similarly small team, expect more teams to follow suit. The L.A. Lakers, for example, passed on 6'11" (2.1 m) center Jahlil Okafor in the 2015 NBA draft to take 6'5" (2 m) shooting guard D'Angelo Russell instead. The Lakers are a team with a tradition of big men being central to championships, from Mikan, Chamberlain, and Abdul-Jabbar to O'Neal and Pau Gasol. But given the way the game is developing, L.A. decided to go small. Small ball is looking like the trend of the future in the NBA.

BEHIND THE ARC

The three-point line has existed in the NBA since 1979, but the 23-foot (7-m) jump shot rarely has been viewed as the best option for the offense. That old-school way of thinking is shifting as well. Teams recently have begun to rely on the jumper from beyond the three-point line as an essential part of their offensive strategy. The NBA average for three-point shots in a game in 2015 was 22.5. That number would have led the league 15 years earlier. Teams have embraced the bomb, and for those who use it strategically, the numbers bear them out.

Using the 2013-2014 season as an example, the NBA average for shots inside the **arc** was 48.8 percent, including layups and dunks. That yield is just 0.98 points per shot. To break even from beyond the arc, the average would need to be less than 33 percent. The league average from the three-point range that season was 36 percent. The math does not lie. Running an offense to get as many good looks from the three-point range as possible is an empirically sound strategy, and more and more coaches have taken note. Bombs away!

NO REWARD FOR MEDIOCRITY

The current NBA playoff format, where the top eight teams from each conference qualify for the postseason, has been in place since 1984. The format draws criticism in years when the Eastern and Western Conferences are not competitively balanced, resulting in teams with sub-.500 records qualifying in one conference, while teams with winning records are left out in the other.

The possible solution that has been suggested is to have the division winners automatically qualify and then seed the next 10 best teams.

NEW RULES

Other rule changes that have been discussed or implemented as a trial in the developmental league include:

- Letting division winners keep a top four playoff seedings regardless of record

- Calling intentional fouls when a team repeatedly fouls the opponent's worst free throw shooter

- Reducing the free agent moratorium period from eight days

- Giving coaches challenges to contest questionable calls

American Airlines Arena, Miami Heat

Toyota Center, Houston Rockets

TD Garden, Boston Celtics

United Center, Chicago Bulls

Moda Center, Portland Trail Blazers

Staples Center, Los Angeles Lakers & Clippers

FUTURE STARS

The New Orleans Hornets took Kentucky big man Anthony Davis with the first overall pick in 2012. Davis has the makings of a possible all-time great. In his first season in New Orleans, he averaged more than 13 points and eight rebounds per game to finish second in Rookie of the Year voting behind Damian Lillard. For the next season, the Hornets changed the team name to Pelicans, and the 6'10" (2.1 m) Davis became a dominant force on defense. He led the league in blocks per game and averaged more than 20 points and 10 rebounds. He repeated the trick the following season, which got Davis named to the All-Star Team.

Canadian-born Andrew Wiggins was the first overall pick in the 2014 NBA draft, taken by Cleveland. The Cavaliers then traded Wiggins to Minnesota as part of a three-way deal involving six players, including Kevin Love, who went the other way in the trade. Wiggins rewarded the Timberwolves with a Rookie of the Year performance in the 2014-2015 season. The 6'8" (2 m) Wiggins averaged 16.9 points and 4.6 rebounds per game and has all the qualities of a surefire star.

Anthony Davis

Andrew Wiggins

HOOP DREAMS

From inner-city playgrounds to makeshift courts in Indiana barns, basketball is played across the country and, increasingly, the world. Every day, kids pick up a ball dreaming of being the next Lebron James or Stephen Curry. America's homegrown sport has come a long way, and its future is bright.

Text-Dependent Questions:

1. What is a possible solution that has been suggested to solve the criticism over the current NBA playoff format, where the top eight teams from each conference qualify for the postseason?

2. Name two new rule changes that have been discussed or implemented as a trial in the developmental league.

3. Which up-and-coming star in his first season in New Orleans averaged more than 13 points and eight rebounds per game to finish second in Rookie of the Year?

Research Project:

Study the influence of discussion boards and social media on the modern game, and make your own predictions on what the future holds for basketball based on what you see online in these public forums.

# GLOSSARY OF BASKETBALL TERMS

assist: a pass that directly leads to a teammate making a basket.

blocked shot: when a defensive player stops a shot at the basket by hitting the ball away.

double dribble: when a player dribbles the ball with two hands or stops dribbling and starts again. The opposing team gets the ball.

dribbling: when a player bounces the ball with one hand, either standing still or moving.

field goal: a successful shot worth two points—three points if shot from behind the three-point line.

foul: called by the officials for breaking a rule: reaching in, blocking, charging, and over the back, for example. If a player commits six fouls during the game, he fouls out and must leave play. If an offensive player is fouled while shooting, he usually gets two foul shots (one shot if the player's basket counted or three if he was fouled beyond the three-point line).

foul lane: the area within the end line and foul line, sometimes called "in the paint." Players can only be in the foul lane for three seconds during play and can't be there at all during free throws.

foul shot: a "free throw," an uncontested shot taken from the foul line (15 feet [4.6 m]) from the basket.

goaltending: when a defensive player touches the ball after it has reached its highest point on the way to the basket. The team on offense gets the points they would have received from the basket. Goaltending is also called on any player, on offense or defense, who slaps the backboard or touches the ball directly above the basket.

jump ball: when an official puts the ball into play by tossing it in the air. Two opposing players try to tip it to their own teammate.

man-to-man defense: when each defensive player guards a single offensive player.

officials: those who monitor the action and call fouls. In the NBA there are three for each game.

position: where each of the five players on the team plays. The most common lineup has two guards, two forwards, and a center.

point guard: the player who handles the ball most on offense. He brings the ball up the court and tries to create scoring opportunities through passing. Good point guards are quick, good passers and can see the court well.

shooting guard: a player whose main job is to score using jump shots and drives to the basket. Good shooting guards are usually taller than point guards but still quick.

small forward: a player whose main job is to score from inside or outside. Good small forwards are taller than point or shooting guards and have speed and agility.

power forward: a player whose main jobs are to score from close to the basket and win offensive and defensive rebounds. Good power forwards are tall and strong.

center: a player whose main job is to score near the basket and win offensive and defensive rebounds. Centers are usually the tallest players on the court, and the best are able to move with speed and agility.

rebound: when a player gains possession of the ball after a missed shot.

roster: the players on a team. NBA teams have 12-player rosters.

shot clock: a 24-second clock that starts counting down when a team gets the ball. The clock restarts whenever the ball changes possession. If the offense does not shoot the ball in time, it turns the ball over to the other team.

steal: when a defender takes the ball from an opposing player.

technical foul: called by the official for misconduct or a procedural violation. The team that does not commit the foul gets possession of the ball and a free throw.

three-point play: a two-point field goal combined with a successful free throw. This happens when an offensive player makes a basket but is fouled in the process.

three-point shot: a field goal made from behind the three-point line.

traveling: when a player moves, taking three steps or more, without dribbling, also called "walking." The opposing team gets the ball.

turnover: when the offensive team loses the ball: passing the ball out of bounds, traveling, or double dribbling, for example.

zone defense: when each defensive player guards within a specific area of the court. Common zones include 2-1-2, 1-3-1, or 2-3. Zone defense has only recently been allowed in the NBA.

CHRONOLOGY

1891 The game of basketball is invented by Dr. James Naismith of Springfield, Massachusetts.

1895 The scoring system of two points for a field goal and one point for a free throw is adopted.

1896 The first professional game is played in Trenton, New Jersey.

1896 The first intercollegiate women's game is played between Stanford and Cal.

1926 Abe Saperstein creates the Harlem Globetrotters.

1936 Basketball is introduced as an Olympic sport at the Summer Games in Berlin, Germany.

1949 The three-year-old Basketball Association of America and National Basketball League merge to form the 17-team National Basketball Association.

1954 The NBA adopts the shot clock.

1961 Wilt Chamberlain rewrites the NBA record book by scoring 100 points in a regulation game.

1966 Texas Western beats Kentucky to win the NCAA tournament using five black starters.

1967 The American Basketball Association starts play; in 1976 it folds, and four teams join the NBA.

1968 The Naismith Basketball Hall of Fame opens in Springfield, Massachusetts.

1972 The L.A. Lakers win 33 straight regular-season games.

1979 The NBA adopts the three-point shot.

1984 Kareem Abdul-Jabbar passes Wilt Chamberlain on the career-scoring list.

1992 In the first Olympic Games since International Basketball Federation (FIBA) changed the rules to allow professionals to play for their country, the United States forms the "Dream Team," the greatest team ever assembled, and wins gold.

1995 John Stockton passes Magic Johnson as the career assists leader.

1996 The Chicago Bulls win a record 72 regular-season games.

1997 The WNBA plays its first game.

2008 Boston beats the Lakers for its 17th NBA title in franchise history, the most of all-time.

2009 University of Tennessee women's coach Pat Summitt gets win number 1,000.

2011 The start of the NBA season is delayed until Christmas Day due to the fourth lockout in league history.

NBA Today: In 2015-2016 the Golden State Warriors had one of the greatest seasons in NBA history. The team broke the record 72 wins accumulated by Michael Jordan's 1995-1996 Chicago Bulls by winning 73 games. The Warriors were led by 2015 league MVP Stephen Curry, who that season became the first player in history to make more than 400 three-point baskets. He broke his own three-point shooting record, set the previous season, as he continued to establish himself as the best shooter of all time.

FURTHER READING:

Indovino, Shaina. *Lebron James (Superstars in the World of Basketball).* Broomall, PA: Mason Crest, 2014

Dayton, Connor. *Kobe Bryant: NBA Scoring Sensation (Living Legends of Sports).* New York: Rosen Education Service, 2015

Editors of Sports Illustrated. *Sports Illustrated Basketball's Greatest: 2014.* New York: Sports Illustrated, 2014.

Kelley, K.C. *Basketball Superstars 2015 (NBA Readers).* New York: Scholastic Paperback Nonfiction, 2015.

INTERNET RESOURCES:

National Basketball Association: http://www.nba.com

ESPN NBA: http://www.espn.go/nba

Basketball Reference: http://www.basketball-reference.com/

Naismith Memorial Basketball Hall of Fame: http://www.hoophall.com/

VIDEO CREDITS:

Wilt Scores 100 (pg 8) https://www.youtube.com/watch?v=TuIM9pWRPBo

Havlicek's Steal (pg 9) http://www.nba.com/video/channels/nba_tv/2015/04/10/1965-east-finals-havlicek-steals-the-ball.nba/

Reed Plays Hurt (pg 10) http://www.nba.com/video/channels/nba_tv/2015/05/08/20150508-gt-willis-reed-return-1970-050815-v2.nba/

Magic Starts at Center (pg 11) http://www.nba.com/video/channels/nba_tv/2015/05/15/historic-content-magic-johnson-1980-nba-finals-gm6-features-v2.nba/

Bird Robs Detroit (pg 12) https://www.youtube.com/watch?v=Wp_gpLSUMRI

Magic's Baby Hook (pg 13) https://www.youtube.com/watch?v=R8-FO57_fvU

Jordan Hits "The Shot" (pg 14) http://www.nba.com/video/channels/nba_tv/2015/05/07/20150507-the-shot-mj-over-ehlo-mix.nba/

Jordan Beats the Jazz (pg 15) https://www.youtube.com/watch?v=PRCTp57LQro

QR CODES AND LINKS TO THIRD-PARTY CONTENT

You may gain access to certain third-party content ("Third-Party Sites") by scanning and using the QR Codes that appear in this publication (the "QR Codes"). We do not operate or control in any respect any information, products, or services on such Third-Party Sites linked to by us via the QR Codes included in this publication, and we assume no responsibility for any materials you may access using the QR Codes. Your use of the QR Codes may be subject to terms, limitations, or restrictions set forth in the applicable terms of use or otherwise established by the owners of the Third-Party Sites. Our linking to such Third-Party Sites via the QR Codes does not imply an endorsement or sponsorship of such Third-Party Sites, or the information, products, or services offered on or through the Third- Party Sites, nor does it imply an endorsement or sponsorship of this publication by the owners of such Third-Party Sites.

PICTURE CREDITS

INDEX

In this index, page numbers in **bold italics** font indicate photos or videos.

INDEX